e Data

Poodles

ELIZABETH NOLL

WORLD BOOK

BOLT

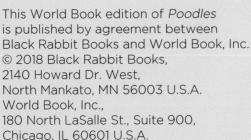

This World Book edition of *Poodles*
is published by agreement between
Black Rabbit Books and World Book, Inc.
© 2018 Black Rabbit Books,
2140 Howard Dr. West,
North Mankato, MN 56003 U.S.A.
World Book, Inc.,
180 North LaSalle St., Suite 900,
Chicago, IL 60601 U.S.A.

Jennifer Besel, editor; Grant Gould, interior designer; Michael Sellner,
cover designer; Omay Ayres, photo researcher

Library of Congress Control Number: 2016049958

ISBN: 978-0-7166-9327-7

Printed in the United States at CG Book Printers,
North Mankato, Minnesota, 56003. 3/17

Image Credits
Alamy: De Meester Johan,
10 (full page); david sanger, 16; Ian
Rutherford, 17 (walking); Tierfotoagentur /
K. Luehrs, 6–7, 19 (bottom), 27; Dreamstime:
Andrey Burmakin, 14; Jajaladdawan, 23 (senior);
iStock: MCCAIG, 19 (top); Shutterstock: Accent, 10
(standard); Baronb, 16; Dora Zett, 8–9; Eric Isselee,
18–19 (most popular dogs), 28; Eudyptula, 12–13;
HelgaMariah, 11 (left); Juha Saastamoinen, 24–25; Lim
Tiaw Leong, Cover, 18 (full page), 32; Lucky Business,
21; Lumppini, 4–5; Mark Herreid, 31; pavla, 23 (adult);
sf2301420max, 3; SungHee_Kang, 15; tsik, 23 (adolescent); vectorstockstoker, 11 (right); Wilson's Vision, 1,
Back Cover
Every effort has been made to contact copyright
holders for material reproduced in this
book. Any omissions will be rectified in
subsequent printings if notice is
given to the publisher.

Contents

CHAPTER 1

Meet the

Poodle

It was after midnight. A boy and his family were sleeping. Suddenly, the family's dog went crazy. Their poodle barked and barked. The barking woke the boy.

The boy saw someone through the window. He called 911. The police came. They said someone had robbed a house nearby. But the family's house was safe because of the dog.

Powerful Watchdogs

Poodles are very good watchdogs. They have a great sense of smell. They bark if they don't **recognize** a **scent**.

Poodles are fast and powerful. The dogs are also playful. They love to run and jump.

Poodles are also very smart. Because they are smart, they are easy to train.

WIDE EARS

. . . . .

TAIL

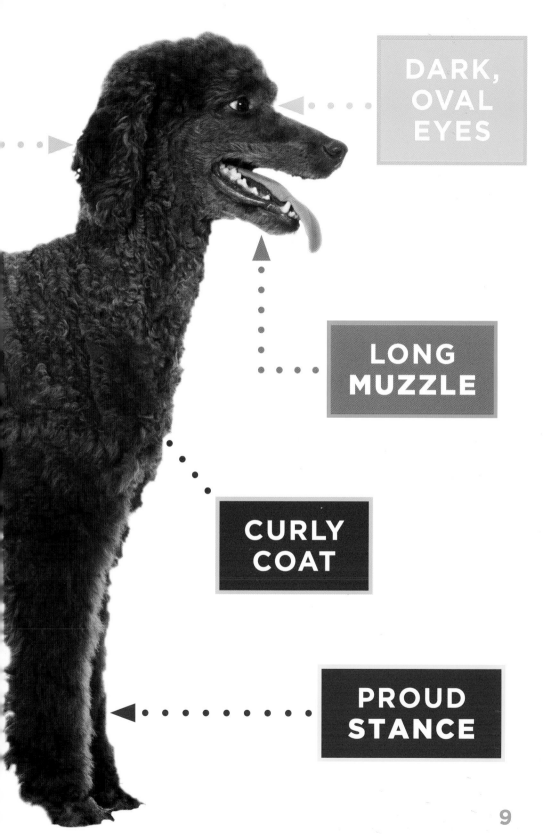

DARK, OVAL EYES

LONG MUZZLE

CURLY COAT

PROUD STANCE

9

15 TO 22 INCHES
(38 to 56 centimeters)

COMPARING HEIGHTS

STANDARD

CHAPTER 2

Poodles'

There are three sizes of poodles. Standard poodles are the biggest. These dogs weigh 45 to 70 pounds (20 to 32 kilograms). A miniature poodle weighs about 15 pounds (7 kg). A toy poodle weighs 9 pounds (4 kg) or less.

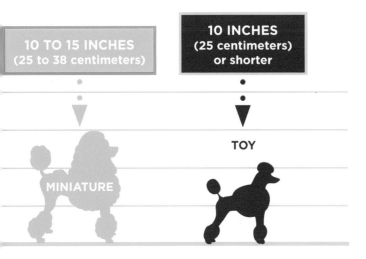

10 TO 15 INCHES (25 to 38 centimeters)

10 INCHES (25 centimeters) or shorter

TOY

MINIATURE

A Poodle Rainbow

Poodles come in many colors. Black is the most common. But poodles can also have white, brown, gray, red, or silver coats.

Poodles don't shed much. Their loose hairs get trapped in their coats instead of falling out.

Thick, curly hair grows all over these dogs. Owners often have groomers cut their poodles' hair. The usual haircut leaves puffs around the ankles. Other body parts are shaved.

Health Problems

Sometimes poodles get sick. They can have problems with their stomachs, **livers**, eyes, or bones. They can also have hip **dysplasia**. • • • • • This problem happens when a dog's hips don't fit together correctly.

CHAPTER 3

A Special

Poodles love to play games. These dogs can learn to play tag, follow the leader, and hide-and-seek.

Poodles have a good sense of humor. They also enjoy **company**. Poodles need lots of attention.

Love to Play

walking

fetching

swimming

TOP 10
MOST POPULAR
Dogs in the United
States in 2015

1
Labrador
Retrievers

2
German
Shepherds

3
Golden
Retrievers

4
Bulldogs

Peace for Poodles

Poodles are calm and peaceful dogs. They don't do well in loud, busy environments. In fact, if poodles' owners fight, the dogs might get sick.

5	6	7	8	9	10
Beagles	French Bulldogs	Yorkshire Terriers	Poodles	Rottweilers	Boxers

CHAPTER 4

Caring for Poodles

All dogs need regular vet checkups. They also need care at home. Poodles need lots of grooming. They need regular baths. They also need to be brushed every day. The dogs also need haircuts about every month. Without haircuts, their hair gets knotted.

Poodle Life Cycle

Newborn poodles are born with their eyes closed.

PUPPY

The smaller poodles become seniors at around eight years old. Standards become seniors at seven years old.

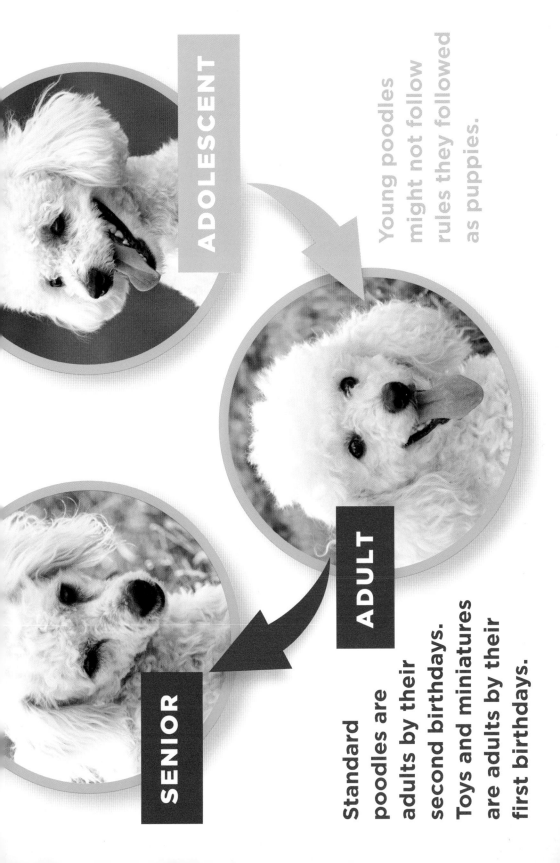

ADOLESCENT

Young poodles might not follow rules they followed as puppies.

ADULT

Standard poodles are adults by their second birthdays. Toys and miniatures are adults by their first birthdays.

SENIOR

Comparing
**Daily
Exercise
Times**

adults

9 months old

3 months old

minutes 0 5 10

Exercising and Eating

All poodles need exercise every day. They need more exercise as they grow up.

All dogs need food and water, of course. Veterinarians help owners decide how much food their dogs should eat.

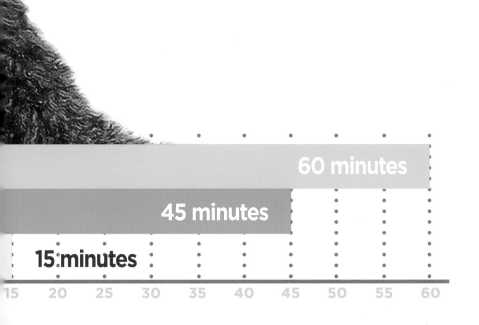

60 minutes

45 minutes

15 minutes

15   20   25   30   35   40   45   50   55   60

Tag a Poodle Today

Poodles are smart, playful dogs. But they do need plenty of attention. They also need grooming every day. But owners say their pups are worth it.

Is a Poodle

Right for You?

Answer the questions below. Then add up your points to see if a poodle is a good fit.

1 **What's your favorite thing to do outside?**

A. sit and read (1 point)

B. ride bike (2 points)

C. play tag with a dog (3 points)

2 How do you feel about brushing a dog?

A. Yuck! **(1 point)**

B. It's OK. **(2 points)**

C. I wish I could do it every day.
(3 points)

3 What kind of coat do you like?

A. smooth and sleek **(1 point)**

B. short and soft **(2 points)**

C. curly and thick **(3 points)**

3 points
A poodle is not your best match.
4–8 points
You like poodles, but another breed might be better for you.
9 points
A poodle would be a great buddy for your life!

GLOSSARY

adolescent (ad-oh-LES-uhnt)—a young person or animal that is developing into an adult

company (KUMP-ne)—someone or something you spend time with or enjoy being with

dysplasia (dys-PLA-zhuh)—an abnormal structure

liver (LIH-vuhr)—an organ in the body

muzzle (MUH-zuhl)—the usually long nose and mouth of an animal

recognize (REH-keg-niz)—to know and remember someone or something

scent (SENT)—a smell that is left by an animal or person

stance (STANS)—a way of standing

BOOKS

Berry, Breanna. *Poodles.* Awesome Dogs. Minneapolis: Bellwether Media, 2016.

Bodden, Valerie. *Poodles.* Fetch! Mankato, MN: Creative Education, 2014.

Johnson, Jinny. *Poodle.* My Favorite Dog. Mankato, MN: Smart Apple Media, 2013.

WEBSITES

Poodle Club of America
www.poodleclubofamerica.org

Poodle Dog Breed Information
www.akc.org/dog-breeds/poodle/

Poodle (Standard) Guide
www.animalplanet.com/breed-selector/dog-breeds/non-sporting/poodle-standard.html

INDEX